M000302234

Roots

and

Wings

A Collection of Poems Inspired by the Truth in the Trees

Lisa Kahl

Halo
PUBLISHING
INTERNATIONAL

Copyright © 2018 Lisa Kahl
All rights reserved.

No part of this book may be reproduced in any manner without the written consent of the publisher except for brief excerpts in critical reviews or articles.

ISBN: 978-1-61244-701-8
Library of Congress Control Number: 2018912531

Printed in the United States of America

Published by Halo Publishing International
1100 NW Loop 410
Suite 700 - 176
San Antonio, Texas 78213
1-877-705-9647
www.halopublishing.com
contact@halopublishing.com

In deep gratitude and devotion,

These words and wings are dedicated and set free...

For hummingbird, butterfly, and bear,

Ireland, Anam Cara, and God.

CONTENTS

Introduction

On June 22, 2017, while hiking the Dingle Peninsula in beloved Ireland, I heard the voice of God. It was audible, clear, resolute. "You have to trust," He said. "You have to trust."

It was time to step away from my place of work, make space for Him to carve a new path, and create a fresh start.

Gratefully, I had reached a point in my life where listening to that voice trumped dismissing it. Upon returning to Cleveland, I took a leap of faith and moved on. To where, to what, to whom I did not know, and yet I felt content. I entered a quiet, reflective period wholly dependent on God's lead that I was willing to follow.

I went for a walk. And then a drive. And then another walk. And another drive. I immersed myself, exploring roads and trails that were covered by a canopy of trees big and small. As time went by, I found myself hypnotized by a story unfolding in the foliage. Step by step, day after day, I became empowered with a heart to see the truth in every branch and tree.

I felt compelled to pen their touching tales—the least I could do in return for the peace and protection they offered me daily. To my surprise, poems surfaced, word by word, laced together by a free spirit and the guidance of God. With ease and abandon, the trees' lessons of life found a home in my journals. And there I believed they would stay. Until heaven whispered again, "They are to be shared."

At that moment, I realized these poems were designed with a purpose after all. Divinely born, they were meant to console a heart, to fashion a bond, to forge the framework of a friendship. To be a gift of the soul, for a soul. Shyly, I set the first poem free, the timing of its delivery immaculate. A sign I was on the right track. Its recipient not only was moved and appreciative but also encouraging, inspiring more poems. Abundantly, in the giving, came the receiving. In a single breath, it dawned on me. Deep down, I am a writer. I am a gift of God. I am a voice that matters and a vessel of His Word, His light, His love.

As I write these very words, I sit and rest in the hand of God, the tree on the cover of this book. This is the tree that holds the most meaning of all, the tree that bequeathed the greatest strength and an ever-lasting memory. One week after writing his story, he came crashing down. Many who walked his trail felt they had lost an old friend. Perhaps once his story had been told and his destiny fulfilled, it was time to return to Source. His trunk now splays across the river; he has become a bridge to the other side. And with his fallen state came a shift in perspective. Two fresh images unearthed. A fish in his trunk and a kiss in his branches. Albeit bittersweet, the story continued to unfold, complete with the seat in His hand to do my work.

This collection of poems is presented in the order that they were received, honoring the Divine order of life itself. They are birthed from a year in which I was blessed with a grace I could not have imagined, strengthened by a seal to follow the call, and awakened to a love I can no longer resist. What follows is a heart surrendered to the current of devotion. . .

Like a breath,
Like a breeze,
Troubles vanish among the trees.

Like Jesus's shadow,
Like love vows made,
Relief is found inside their shade.

Like a teacher,
Like a lark,
Questions answered abreast the bark.
Like a heart played fool,
Like a heart that grieves,
Lessons learned beneath the leaves.

Like a baby born,
Like an awestruck tourist,
There's joy to be found in the frolicking forest.

Like God Himself,
Like a soul stretched limber,
Truth transpires in the thick of timber.

1

STEVE AND SLIM

I spy a partnership. A team of two.

In spite of their contrast in stature, they are comrades.

Pilgrims who are always up for adventure and good company.

The younger one yearns to grow. To be worthy of her counterpart.

Yet, their disparity is their true beauty. Perhaps the little one could accept her delicate nature.

Being petite is her strength. Less matter lends more space. . . to be whimsical, feminine, intuitive.

To walk the path of "The Little Way" as St. Therese before her.

Her humility a ladle for gathering souls.

So I say, so I see,

Effortlessly taught by a tree.

Born 11/11/17

2

J & B

I spy two lovers and the space between them. Distance only
years can create.

Years of withheld and mismanaged words. Layers of blame and
resentment for dreams gone by.

One inches one way, one inches the other. Gradually, a cavern
so grave, a reunion seems inconceivable.

The demand for a fresh outlook rests solely on them. If only
one could see.

To flip their image upside down, they are truly a pair of wings.
Yoked together to sense harmony.

Disembodied enough to remain unique. Discord gives way to
relief and gratitude.

As they are humbly reminded, it takes two wings to fly!

Let it go, let it be,
Effortlessly taught by a tree.
Born 11/14/17

3

THE BURNING BUSH

I spy the burning bush, a sign that God is near,

Fervent red and ardent orange, shades that God is clear.

He speaks to me through tendered leaves, just around the bend,

His Word is firm and resolute, His message mine to tend.

Heart aflame, His voice proclaims—

"You have a light, you cannot hide,

Fulfill My call, fill Me with pride.

I choose you to live as I,

To be My breath, My love, My eye.

Trumpet My Way, blazon the trail,

Acclaim the birth of Lisa Kahl.

For the Kingdom quakes and the birds call out,

When one so brave entrusts My route.

Open their eyes to every storm, My Presence in its truest form.

I dwell in every bush they see,

In the weeds, the wind, the honeybee.

It is the truth, it is to be,

Effortlessly taught by a tree.

Born 11/20/17

4

THE DRAGON ELLE

I spy longing. I sense loss. A hollow heart, once suffused with possibility, now teeming with despair.

She hungers for her mate, a companion who formerly bridged the road, stemming from the other side.

Together they offered shelter and guidance to believers below.

Two kindred limbs, one congruent mission. Although robbed of touch, bound by a shared story.

It is said they breathed fire, a pair of dragons in the sky! A desperate endeavor to explore each other's heat.

Sadly, fate blew in. The form of a storm. He succumbed to its fury, barely time to say goodbye.

Dutifully, she carries on. Propelled by obedience and service.

Nevertheless, her soul remains suspended in time. . . with him.

Love's mark, love's memory,
Effortlessly taught by a tree.
Born 11/23/17

5

Puff the Magic Dragon

I spy a dragon. A lover's grave.

Born from the battlefield, a youth of wood and river
matured into a noble being.

A sagacious spirit, dedicated servant, and eagle-eyed
guardian who endlessly blessed all in his path.

He spent a lifetime poised above a road of weary travelers
only to be returned to the forest.

Nestled deep in the thicket, he remains regal even in death.

Although at rest, he is a statuesque creature who sustains
his sight. An open eye, awaiting his beloved, the one who
shares his devotion for shielding souls.

A definitive mark stitched to his mane echoes the depiction
of his dearest's symbol. An anchor she was, and in his sudden
demise so was he branded with her emblem.

A badge to stake her claim, a kiss to console his heart. . .
Until they meet again.

Love fiercely, love truly,
Effortlessly taught by a tree.
Born 12/10/17

6

THE HAMMER

I spy a hammer. A carpenter's muse.

A craftsman's instrument to forge a manifestation of the heart.
Passed from man to man, teacher to apprentice, father to son,
the tool carries a legacy all its own.

Surely if granted speech, it would say, "At last, I'm with the
one. I lie on a table of freedom, a home to rouse my finest offering.
Peering up from the workbench, the gaze of a profound artist
penetrates me.

I am engulfed by mesmerizing eyes of tenderness tempered
with strength.

Slow and steady, he grasps my handle and I sense a belonging.
Draped in a palm of truth, rough edges soften to his will.

Wholly consumed in the grip of grace, cleansed and cleared by
ripples of peace and love.

Hands of light upon me, inspiration trickles in. . . to yield,
serve, bear fruit.
Steel and wood burn desire and forevermore declare—
In his hands, beneath his breath, about his body, along his soul,
I am meant to be.
From a distance rings the call of a gentle mother for suppertime.
Our work ceases. Incarcerated in my box, I patiently await the
return of my partner, my friend, my maker."

In His hands, thy life be,
Effortlessly taught by a tree.
Born 12/25/17

7
THE PORTRAIT

I spy a portrait. A lane of love.

A kindled heart to illume the way.

It beckons to be seen, reached, touched.

Throbs to be lived in, appreciated, and adored.

Aches to be equaled in depth and sensibility.

Yearns to inspire, liberate, purify. An awareness dawns.

In wordless surrender, I drift toward a mirror image of myself.

An evening stroll becomes a path of passion and purpose.

Drawn by a chord of recognition, a quickening of step, I am
enraptured and aroused by this velvet curtain's plea.

Thunder feet devour a seductive route to reciprocity.

Each stride fortifies a practice, forsaking contemplation,
knowing a brighter bond beams afar. I press on—

Pining to find respite in unification and apricity at the
journey's end.

Casting all cares on a safe passage home. Upon fusing, a deep-
seated craving at last satisfied.

Finally in true communion, forever released of all that came
before.

Seek symmetry, seek harmony,

Effortlessly taught by a tree.

Born 12/26/17

8
UBUNTU

I spy a teepee. On a tenebrous night.

Sent by the winds of change, I quietly stand by the door.

Legend proclaims a medicine man dwells within.

A healer of hearts.

A lover of life.

For it is said his is a house of God, his technique abundant love.

Trembling with trepidation, I conjure courage to enter.

I breathe in.

I breathe out.

Reluctantly, my soul steps forward.

Crossing the threshold,

Seized and softened by an undertow of tranquility.

Wrapped in the skin of something greater,

Sheltered and supported by a structure of truth.

Face to face, we sit. Bare, brilliant, blessed.

Generosity of attention and presence prove stronger than any words spoken.

Beholden, my body quivers to be seen, be felt, be alive!

Inside his frame, I grow two inches. Life glistens and there is joy in every breath.

Renewed, my soul steps away. Healed, whole and a vessel of God's love.

Surrendered, serene, and surrounded by God's beauty.

This is the Way, you will see,

Effortlessly taught by a tree.

Born 5/11/18

9
THE WISHBONE

I spy a wish. I see a dream.

Just imagine a place unseen.

With rooted rock and sun so bright,

A definitive space to live in the light.

I hear her calling in the night,

A voice so clear, I sit upright.

"Come to me and be the one,

Spread your joy, inspire fun!

Shine your light, lend a hand,

Minister to God's command.

It is His strength and not your own,

That guides you down a path unknown.

His will, His grace, His boundless love,

Leads you as you rise above.

The fear, the doubt, the darkest hour,

The reckless thoughts, the devil's prowl.

Press on, create, be free, be wild!

All is possible, my child!

Dust off your bones and dive right in,

Immerse your soul in serving Him.

The Shepard hails to heal His flock,

The time is now: tick tock, tick tock.

Be not afraid, be brave, be bold,

Build for Him a city of gold!

You are enough, like Abraham,

God's chosen one, I am, I am.

Wish it so and it shall be,

Effortlessly taught by a tree.

Born 5/18/18

10

THE BROOK COLETTE

I spy a mirror. A sorcerous stream.

An enchanted river, a reflective dream.

Free of ego, age, or shame,

Her waters see in God's own name.

Tenderly drawn to her bank,

I pause to kneel, revere her rank.

Spellbound at the edge of bliss,

She softly whispers for a kiss.

Captivated by her call,

My spirit leans, a forward fall.

Gaze breaks surface, I gasp to see,

My image is a peony.

Flowers strewn on river floor,

Every blink imploring—more.

The creek is blessed to read my heart,

Flavor, essence, set me apart.

Enter the presence behind the veil,

The inner beauty, the truest tale.

With certitude, more than a hunch,
Her current sweeps a beamish bunch.
Daisies, dahlias, daffodils,
Lilacs, lilies, scented thrills.
Every petal, stem, and shade,
Fit to suit my soul's parade.
Fastened by a weed of sea,
Complete, composed, ergo carefree.
Passion and peace my likeness be,
So says the river's chemistry.
Forever in my heart shall stay,
The memory of this brook's bouquet.
To see myself in all my power,
God's little treasure, God's little flower.

Beauty defined in depth and esteem,
Effortlessly taught by a stream.
Born 5/26/18

11

CHARLOTTE

I spy a web. A tethered soul.

A tangled mind, a trammeled body.

An intricate weave of ego's sharp edge.

Woven by worry, wanting, striving, struggle, sabotage.

Fashioned from "not yet", "not enough", "not fair", "not me", "not possible".

Now enslaved by conceited thoughts and desires, paralyzed by one's own self.

Trapped in a maze of resistance, confusion, afflictions, the rage begins to rise.

And rise. And rise.

Restrained for lifetimes, the spirit plots an ambush.

Summons clarity and the courage to act anew.

Now leading from the heart, an escape seems viable.

Sensing the shift, the ego makes a fierce and final cry,

"Push, fight, lash about!

It's the only way through; it's the only way out!"

The tension tightens, the tension dips,

"But today is different," slips from my lips.

Today I see the light through the branches, the light I have so longed to live in.

Today I see the flowers, still and relaxed, allowing life to care for them.

Today I know to follow their call,

For I yearn to be with them, to be like them.

Today I will be silent, stationary, stable,

Content to unravel in God's time and not my own.

Today I see a pasture of promise, of purpose, of peace.

Indeed, today is a new day, a new me, a new life!

Today my story begins. . .

Be still and know you can be free,

Effortlessly taught by a tree.

Born 6/2/18

12
The Hand of God

I spy majesty.
The hand of God up in a tree.
Sovereign in the woods is He,
His presence a true mystery.

Jutting out across the stream,
An anchor in a sea of green.
Rooted, ready to be seen,
To the eye, a poet's dream.

One night while walking on the trail,
God showed Himself in great detail.
'Tis the truth, no old wives' tale,
Sincerity, the Holy Grail.

My stroll to stop when all went silent,
Time stood still beside this giant.
Transported to another place,
Somewhere in time, somewhere in space.

Delivered to the yoga floor,
Stocked with students, I teach, implore,
For strength, courage, balance, breath,

Truth, intention, surrendered death.

Among the pack, one stands out,

His stance, his form, without a doubt,

I recognize that silhouette,

Instinct commands me to protect.

My friend, my teacher, healer, guide,

And partner to stand by my side.

Front and center for all to see,

And yet his soul calls only to me.

"Mountain pose," so I suggest,

A time to touch, be doubly blessed.

Behind him I stand, his back to my chest,

Whole-hearted, supportive, consoling my quest.

Left hand to his heart, his pulse meeting mine,

Graced with a vision of Mercy Divine.

Into his ear, my whisper blows,

"Open your eyes," before the Lord goes.

Before us, Christ is! Before us, Christ gleams!
Warm tears, down our faces in soft, steady streams,
Ever so gently, He takes my friend's hand,
Lifts it to mine, creates a sealed band.
Christ's hand upon his, his hand upon mine,
Bound with intent to heed union from Thine.
The smile of smiles shines on Christ's face!
At last united, His merger in place.

Forthwith two lights to lead the way,
A pair to build God's chief brigade.
One a mountain, one a breeze,
Interlaced, to heal with ease.

Alliance affirms the Trinity,
Effortlessly taught by a tree.
Born 6/6/18

13

A Pisces Soul

I spy a fish. A Pisces soul.

One on which life took its toll.

Burrowed in the burly bark,

She'll purpose pain to leave her mark.

Restrained for years in the abyss,

Writhing, wanting one sweet kiss.

When, O Lord, will I ascend,

Turn a corner, round a bend?

My empathic nature, my romantic heart,

Call out to you for a fresh start!

Scoop me up, protect my being,

Lift me to the sea of seeing.

I need you now, I always have,

Forgive me, Father, apply your salve.

Choose my path, choose my love,

Equal to Your reign above.

Make it worthy, make it grand,

Unique as every grain of sand.

This fluid creature longs to rise,

Accept a challenge, claim her prize!
To see the sun, to breathe the air,
To live her life, without compare.
And then it came, that kiss so sweet,
Not what I thought, yet true, replete.
The kiss of God, amazing grace,
Painted peace upon my face.
Surrendered in His mighty hand,
Courage called to take a stand.
To be the fish who, out of water,
Recognized she was Your daughter.
Unafraid to heed the call,
Be birthed, be seen, be free for all!

God's time, God's grace, God's glory,
Trust in Him to weave your story.
Let it happen, let Him lead,
Effortlessly taught by a tree.
Born 8/3/18

14

RYAN AND KAYLA

I spy connection. I sense relief.
Two kindred limbs in disbelief.
At last they touch, at last they feel,
Something precious, something real.

Years apart on separate sides,
A road of blocks, a great divide.
Their story drifting in the breeze,
Until declared their destinies.

Merely saplings, too young to capture,
One's essence could elicit rapture,
'Twas too soon to feel the power,
To identify their matching flower.

As time went by, as we all do,
Trunks and branches formed and grew.
Inching closer in proximity,
Energized by possibility.

Nearer now to the same city,
Mature enough to seize her, pretty,
Thus, life blew in, life blew out,
Change took its course, fate had its bout.
More time would pass, more spills would fall,

Yet all the while, a steady crawl,
Through lessons learned, in hearts that burned,
Reaching further for all they had yearned.

Then one day it came to be,
Electric touching of tree to tree.
A spark was lit, a full recall,
They knew each other after all.

That moment when you recognize,
Your heart equaled in shape and size.
Home in gaze, tremble in touch,
Thus was born a romance nonesuch.

Unto this one the soul shall sing,
For truth, for love, a sacred ring.
Henceforth two hearts are intertwined,
Bonded, braided, blessed Divine.

So can you see when love's profound,
And fashioned from the King on High,
Its magic yoke and test of time,
Contours a heart up in the sky?

When in the stars, 'tis meant to be,
Effortlessly taught by a tree.
Born 8/5/18

15
The Kiss

I spy a smooch. Love's tender trap.

Walls and limits sure to sap.

Twisted tongues and tickled parts,

Brushstrokes of two souls' fresh starts.

Meshed desire sewn through lips,

Let down in her seasoned hips.

A gateway to the ring of fire,

Life deems we be a multiplier.

Depth of soul in glance and graze,

Captaining each lover's maze.

A homecoming, a bolt of bliss,

Bountifully born from love's first kiss.

Be it French, Eskimo, or butterfly,

Its power one shall not deny.

Inside a kiss, my devotee,

Effortlessly taught by a tree.

Born 8/17/18

16

FALLEN DRAGON

I spy a fallen dragon.
I sense love's fall from grace. . .

Love's fall from grace, a crack in clay,
Love's fall from grace, a grim decay.
Love's fall from grace, to our dismay,
The Lord giveth, the Lord taketh away.

Love's slide, farewell, unwelcome fray,
A wake chockfull, a heavy sleigh,
Disbelief, our tribe astray,
The Lord giveth, the Lord taketh away.

Love's aftermath, assault to the skin,

Oppressive, hollow, life becomes dim,
A sanguine spouse turned divorcee,
The Lord giveth, the Lord taketh away.

Love's memory on the soul to stay,
Tormenting self like Hemingway.
A cry for peace, keep hate at bay,
The Lord giveth, the Lord taketh away.

Love's hills and valleys according to Thee,
Effortlessly taught by a tree.
Born 8/19/18

17

THE TWO-HEADED DRAGON

I spy mayhem,
A duo sublime,
The two-headed dragon,
Disguised in the vine.

A combo so fierce,
Free of earthly desire,
Prepared to take flight,
Transform and conspire.

Fly the sky, skim the sea,
Be the change, plant the seed,
Although two, they are one,
Free to follow God's lead.

Wild in nature,

Mystics at heart,

Force stronger together,

Than if kept apart.

God's creation in love,

God's creation a pair,

Magnets drawn together,

Synergy rare to dare.

Mythical beasts,

Breath of fire inherent,

Burning the world,

Intent truth be transparent.

The power of partnership made clear to me,

Effortlessly taught by a tree.

Born 9/21/18

CPSIA information can be obtained
at www.ICGtesting.com
Printed in the USA
BVHW051456070119
537208BV00007B/214/P

9 781612 447018